VIVA LAS VEGAS

BY:

ANTHONY GORDON PILLA

To order additional copies of this book, contact:

Simply Best Reads LLC
39-67 58th Street, 1st floor
Woodside, NY 11377, USA
Phone: (+1 888-203-7688)
simplybestreads.com

VIVA LAS VEGAS

VIVA LAS VEGAS

VIVA LAS VEGAS

VIVA LAS VEGAS

POLO TOWERS
ARCADE MANIA
Chevys

VIVA LAS VEGAS

VIVA LAS VEGAS

VIVA LAS VEGAS

VIVA LAS VEGAS

LIBERTY DOLLARS

VIVA LAS VEGAS

VIVA LAS VEGAS

VIVA LAS VEGAS

VIVA LAS VEGAS

VIVA LAS VEGAS

VIVA LAS VEGAS

VIVA LAS VEGAS

TREASURE ISLAND
MYSTÈRE
CIRQUE DU SOLEIL

VIVA LAS VEGAS

VIVA LAS VEGAS

VIVA LAS VEGAS

VIVA LAS VEGAS

VIVA LAS VEGAS

VIVA LAS VEGAS

VIVA LAS VEGAS

VIVA LAS VEGAS

$50,000.00*

70's
Slot Tournament
April 13 - 16, 1997

Sunday, April 13th
Registration 10 am to 7 pm
Tournament Orientation 7 pm

Monday, April 14th
Two rounds of play

Tuesday, April 15th
Final rounds of play
Awards Banquet 6:30 pm

Wednesday, April 16th
Departure

VIVA LAS VEGAS

VIVA LAS VEGAS

VIVA LAS VEGAS

VIVA LAS VEGAS

VIVA LAS VEGAS

VIVA LAS VEGAS

VIVA LAS VEGAS

VIVA LAS VEGAS

VIVA LAS VEGAS

VIVA LAS VEGAS

VIVA LAS VEGAS

VIVA LAS VEGAS

VIVA LAS VEGAS

VIVA LAS VEGAS

VIVA LAS VEGAS

VIVA LAS VEGAS

VIVA LAS VEGAS

VIVA LAS VEGAS

VIVA LAS VEGAS

VIVA LAS VEGAS

VIVA LAS VEGAS

VIVA LAS VEGAS

VIVA LAS VEGAS

VIVA LAS VEGAS

VIVA LAS VEGAS

VIVA LAS VEGAS

VIVA LAS VEGAS

VIVA LAS VEGAS

NEVADA
RENO
LAS VEGAS